"Musicality for Social Dancing"

Filling in the Blanks of Argentine Tango
- Book Seven -

Oliver Kent PhD

Also By Oliver Kent PhD

Enjoy Getting the Dances You Want – Filling in the Blanks of Argentine Tango Book 1

Understanding the Mystery of the Embrace Part 1 – Filling in the Blanks of Argentine Tango Book 2

Understanding the Mystery of the Embrace Part 2 – Filling in the Blanks of Argentine Tango Book 3

The Art of Leading and Following - Conducción to Intención - Filling in the Blanks of Argentine Tango Book 4

Understanding Musicality: "Al Compás del Corazón": Filling in the Blanks of Argentine Tango - Book 5

Understanding Musicality Dinámica y Sincopación: Filling in the Blanks of Argentine Tango - Book 6

Inspirational Buddhist Quotations - Meditations and Reflection Book 1

Inspirational Buddhist Quotations - Meditations and Reflections Book 2

Finding Hope : Searching for Happiness Book 1

Beginners Guide to Meditation: How to Start Meditating An Easy, Practical Guide

All rights reserved. No part of this book may be reproduced in any form without permission in writing from the publisher, except in the case of brief quotations embodied in critical articles or reviews.

Although the author and publisher have made every effort to ensure that the information in this book was correct at the time of publishing, the author and publisher do not assume and hereby disclaim any liability to any party for any loss, damage, or disruption caused by errors or omissions, whether such errors or omissions result from negligence, accident, or any other cause.

This book is not intended as a substitute for the medical advice of physicians.

The information in this book is meant to supplement, not replace, proper training. Like any activity involving speed, equipment, balance and environmental factors, tango poses some inherent risk. The authors and publisher advise readers to take full responsibility for their safety and know their limits. When practicing the skills described in this book, do not take risks beyond your level of experience, aptitude, training, and comfort level.

Copyright © 2019 Oliver Kent
All rights reserved
ISBN 9781709637285

Illustrations by Oscar B Frise

Dedicated to Natasha for "sound effects"

Table of Contents

About the Author xi
    Referring to Previous Books in the Series xiii
Video and Music Clips..xv
A brief note on the illustrations xvii
    A quick overview of moves xviii
    Free and Weighted Legs xix
    Boleo (boh-LAY-oh) xx
Cuddle-shuffling xxii
Introduction 1
Chapter 1 Many Ways Up the Mountain 3
    The Wrong Mountain 5
    Mount Choerography 6
    De-cluttering 7
    The McTest 8
    Choreography 10
    Advanced Fundamentals 10
    Summary 13
Chapter 2 Musical Punctuation.............................15
    Terminology – Musical Genre.....................16
    The Witching Hour 16
    Terminology – Punctuation 17
    Emphasis 18
Starting to find your way with the Musical Cues 19
How Cues Punctuate the Music 21
Exercise 1 22

    Feeling the Phrases 23
        Exercise 2 24
        Troubleshooting 25
    Summary 26
Chapter 3 Rhythmic Punctuation 29
    Exercise 3 30
    Exercise 4 31
    The 'Five' 32
        Exercise 5 33
    The End of a Verse 33
        Exercise 6 33
        Troubleshooting 34
    Sharp Turn Ahead! 34
        Statement of the 'Obvious' 1 35
        Exercise 7 35
    Don't Miss Your Exit 37
    Synergies 38
    I Don't Think We're in Kansas any More 39
    Summary 41
Chapter 4 La Cumparsita 43
    La Cumparsita: Part 1 44
        Exercise 8 44
    The Vanishing Compás 45
    La Cumparsita: Part 2 46
    La Cumparsita: Part 3 49
    Summary 51
Chapter 5 Melody 53
    Exercise 9 55

- Exercise 10 55
- Exercise 11 57
- But how do you know which notes to step on?. 59
- Exercise 12 59
- Levels of Emphasis 60
- 'Rises' 61
  - Exercise 13 62
  - Exercise 14 62
  - Exercise 15 64
  - Exercise 16 65
- Exercise 17 66
- Summary 67
- Chapter 6 Lyrics and Poetry 69
  - Statement of the 'Obvious' 2 70
  - Statement of the 'Obvious' 3 71
  - Exercise 18 71
  - Exercise 19 72
  - Troubleshooting 72
  - Exercise 20 72
- When the Compás is Missing in Action 73
  - Exercise 21 73
  - Exercise 22 79
- Breaking it down 79
- "You're not the Boss of Me!" 81
- Cruising 83
  - Exercise 23 83
- The "Right" Way 84
  - Exercise 24 86

- Exercise 25 86
- Summary 89
- Chapter 7 Lyrics, Melody and Rhythm 91
  - Precognition 93
  - 'Call and Response' 95
  - Exercise 26 95
  - Light and Shade 99
  - 'Heartbeat and Color' 102
  - Bahia Blanca 103
    - Exercise 27 103
    - Exercise 28 105
  - When is a Burger no longer a Burger? 105
  - Summary 107
- Epilogue 109
- Statements of the 'Obvious' 113
- Terminology 113

About the Author

Oliver Kent has been dancing all his life and Argentine Tango for longer than he can remember. He's noticed that there are a lot of "blanks" in the way tango is usually taught that you're supposed to fill in by dancing socially. Unfortunately this doesn't always work that well and many find themselves making slow progress, or stuck on a plateau.

Oliver's experience and ability to coherently explain these details is regularly sought out by dancers from all over the world, from those just getting their feet wet, to established teachers.

He originally intended to write a book filling in the blanks, enabling others to become good social dancers. He then realized he'd underestimated just how many blanks there were!

The book became a trilogy, which in turn became a series.

Referring to Previous Books in the Series

It's surprising just how many Blanks there are to Fill in for becoming a Good Social Dancer! Although I realize some will read these books out of order or only read a few of them, they are intended to be read as a series.

Each book builds on the next.

If you can't actually get any dances, then everything else is academic. Hence the first book focuses on this. A good tango posture and embrace makes actual dancing so much easier – this is covered in Books 2 and 3.

Then ideally, you need to be able to lead and/or follow in a connected, comfortable way that allows you to move freely.

After that, being able to dance with the music, makes life a lot easier.

To avoid repeating massive amounts of previous books, I will simply refer to them in the text like this (Book 1.)

You don't need to have read any of my other books

in order to use this one. If you're content that you have a grasp of musicality already – or that the one you have is good enough for now – then you can certainly use that to practice the ideas in this book.

If you're not sure, you should at least be comfortable with these ideas:

The first beat of any song is the "One." Simply because you start counting "**One**, two, three..."

Tango music is then usually broken down into groups of either four or eight beats, called phrases. Again, the first beat of each phrase is also considered to be the 'One.'

For this book, you should be able to find the 'One' and the 'Compás', the underlying beat. See Book 5, Understanding Musicality: "Al Compás del Corazón", if you're struggling.

My intention is to write in a way that if you have read my other books you'll gain extra insight; not to make parts of the book inaccessible if you haven't.

Video and Music Clips

Although pictures help, there's no real substitute for being able to hear music and see it being played.

I reference a number of video and songs in this book. At the time of writing, things are a bit up in the air regarding copyright. A large number of Youtubers are considering a Class Action Suit against some of the bigger music companies for what they feel is a breach of their legal right to Fair Use.

It looks like Youtube has reached some kind of compromise by adding a link to an official source for any video that contains copyrighted material. But the future remains uncertain.

Youtube itself may cease to exist – it has somehow consistently failed to make a profit.

I try to choose videos that have been up for years. Although it's the essential nature of the internet to ebb and flow, a video that's been up for six years is not likely to come down now.

Where necessary, I've added suggestions for how to find similar videos, should any of the ones I've referenced be taken down.

Regarding tango music, in the US, after 50 years music enters the Public Domain and loses it's copyright status. Given that 95% of tango music was written before 1950, that's most of it. Certainly everything I've referred to in this book.

Generally, searching for the artist and the song on Youtube will find you the track. For more recent artists, I've included links to any official videos they artists have posted. You can also buy the songs from "all good music stores" either digitally or, if you have something that will play them, on cds and even records!

All material referenced in this book is done so under Fair Use for Educational Purposes. No infringement of copyright is intended or should be implied. I categorically don't own any of these works.

A brief note on the illustrations

The illustrations in this book are there to guide you.

None of these illustrations are intended to be something that you copy exactly. They're illustrative rather than prescriptive. Don't worry about the precise angle the model's knee is at.

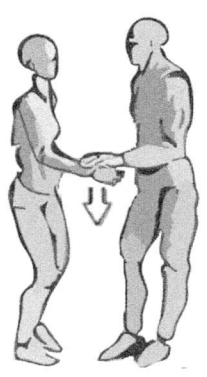

A quick overview of moves

While this is no means an extensive list of tango moves - to aid the flow of the book - I'm going to give a brief explanation of some. While each has a lot of variations, this is enough for these purposes.

These are intended for you if don't know these moves, so don't worry. I refer to them in the book, but you won't need to actually be able to do them yet. Any teacher or experienced dancer will be able to demonstrate these moves in a few seconds, if you ask them nicely.

Free and Weighted Legs

The 'free leg' is the one you aren't standing on. Whereas, the 'weighted leg' is the one you are standing on.

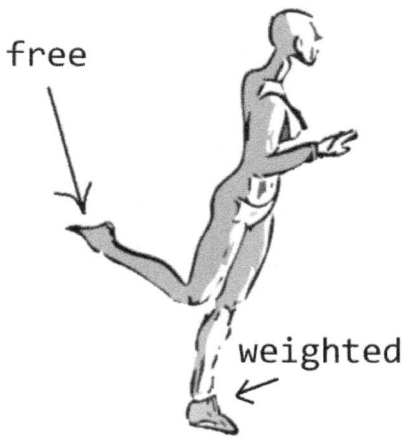

Boleo (boh-LAY-oh)

A graceful arcing movement of the free leg. It can be behind the follower,

or in front

Cuddle-shuffling

Dancing only using weight-changes and shuffling around. Usually done in close embrace - an effective way to accelerate your progress (Book 3)

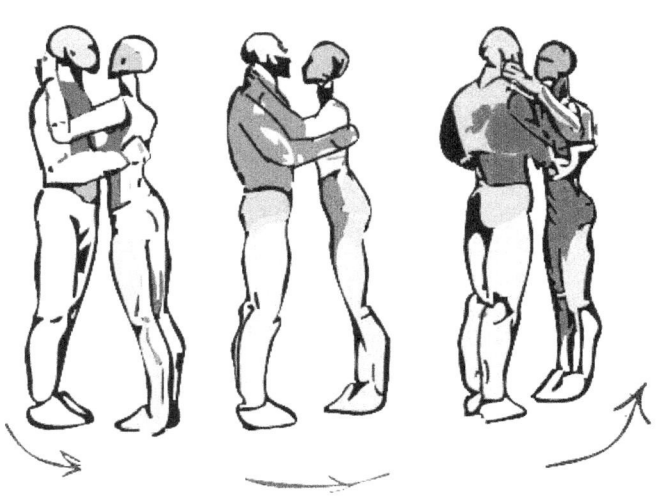

Introduction

"What is it you're not doing?" ~ *Nathan Fillion*

One of the best contrasts between musicality in choreography and in social dancing, is from an out-take from the film "Serenity."

In a magnificent performance, the two main characters - "Mal" and "The Operative" - are squaring off, setting up the conflict that will drive the rest of the film. Meanwhile, Morena Baccarin's character "Inara", is supposed to be doing something sneaky with a prop. When Mal, played by Nathan Fillion, asks her

"What are you doing?"

Inara's supposed to hint at how she's soon going to save them both from the Bad Guy.

Unfortunately, while the character of Inara is supposed to concerned about helping Mal, Morena is lost in the moment, watching this scene unfold. She's definitely not thinking ahead to what her character's actually meant to be doing.

When Nathan turns to her to deliver his line, he

discovers that instead of sneaking around with props, she's simply standing still, transfixed by the performance.

He calmly – and somewhat snarkily - changes his line to

*"What is it you're **not** doing?"*

She blinks in confusion, followed by realization, and the spell breaks.

When you're dancing choreography, you want to be Nathan. But for social dancing, you want to be Morena, lost in the moment as you dance. However, given the complexity within Argentine Tango's music, how can you dance musically, without needing to think..?

Chapter 1 Many Ways Up the Mountain

"There are many paths leading to the top of Mount Fuji."

~ *Morihei Ueshiba*

Each time you dance Argentine Tango, you have the opportunity to create a moment in time that will last forever.

Musicality is one of the secret ingredients to taking your dancing to the next level. It can elevate a collection of simple steps, into a memorable dance.

Thankfully, this can happen as soon as you begin your first dance. Of course, to have a magical first dance, you'll probably need a skilled partner. But then one day, you find that you're the skilled partner creating a magical dance with someone else.

In Book 5, we worked on reliably finding and then moving to the Compás - the underlying rhythm of the music. With this, you can sketch out a picture. Book 6 then built on this, giving an understanding of the different Sincopaciόns and Dinámica; with these you can start to color in your sketch, bringing greater depth and feeling to your dance.

Which brings us to this book, where we ask,

"What elevates a good dance to a great one? One you'll remember a week, a month, a year from now."

By being able to read the subtle signs in the music, you'll react in the moment, feeling your way, rather than needing to plan ahead. By understanding how the orchestra gives you musical cues, you can dance with them, rather than doing your own thing while they happen to be playing.

When you understand the underlying structure and relationships between the rhythm, lyrics and melody, you'll even be able to dance if the Compás goes Missing in Action!

As you discover how to add light and shade to your dancing, you'll start to recognize that musicality is often just as much about what you don't do, bringing greater texture and subtlety to your dance.

By blending these elements together, you come much closer to creating a dance that lasts forever.

The Wrong Mountain

"Climbing the wrong mountain" is one of the biggest problems in social dancing, particularly with musicality.

Imagine Mary and Beth are climbing the same mountain - 'Mount Social Dancing.' Mary has decided to go up the north face, but Beth has chosen to head up the south face. In the same way, two people may be climbing the same mountain of social dancing musicality, but one person approaches it through the Compás, while another focuses on dancing to a specific orchestra.

Although they would appear to be doing completely different things for a while, eventually they'll (hopefully) both meet up again at the top.

Meanwhile, Chloe has started climbing a completely different mountain – 'Mount Choreography.' When she gets to the top of her mountain, she sees Beth and Mary standing on the summit of another mountain! More importantly, she then realizes that the top of their mountain is where she actually wanted to be.

Although the base of the different musicality mountains are roughly the same, the final peaks of musicality for choreography and for social dancing are very different.

Mount Choerography

Choreography is much more cerebral and controlled. First, you decide what it is you want to highlight about your dance; fancy moves, intricate steps, a snuggly embrace? Then you choose music that best shows off how you and your partner do that.

Now you can go through the music in as much detail as you want, phrase by phrase, even note by note if you wish! Gradually you create the dance to go with it, taking into account any other important factors; maybe the stage is a specific shape and size, or you'll need to wear specific clothing? You can change your mind, move pieces of the choreography around, take them out, video the whole thing to see it from different angles and ask other people's opinions.

Then when you finally perform it, you'll spend a lot of your concentration on what's coming next. Both remembering the next moves and setting them up ahead of time.

In fairness, this doesn't mean that it's a lifeless performance. In many ways, it's similar to actors performing on-stage, having to remember their lines, where and when to move and so on.

De-cluttering

"Keep only those things that speak to your heart. Then take the plunge and discard all the rest." ~ Marie Kondo

Social dancing is about being in the moment.

A common theme running through my books is to avoid cluttering your head up with thoughts while you dance - It's better to sort your posture out *before* you even ask someone to dance; that way, you don't have to deal with it when it comes time to focus on embracing them (Book 2.)

While you'll initially need a certain amount of thinking to understand the concepts of social dancing, the aim is to achieve a level where they become intuitive and you no longer need to think about them. If you've ever learned to drive stick shift, you'll know what a nightmare it is to start with.

But in time, you get to a point where changing gears just becomes *driving*, rather than something separate that you have to concentrate on.

The fundamental difference between the two mountains is this:

A choreography will always be filled with thinking ahead. Social dancing, on the other hand, can be danced in the moment.

The McTest

"They f*** you at the drive-thru, okay? They know you're gonna be miles away before you find out you got f***ed!

...I'm not eating the tuna." ~ Leo Getz

How do you make sure you climb the right mountain? Where do things start to go wrong?

At the beginning of both mountains, you first need to understand the basics of how musicality works - knowing the difference between "a beat" and "the beat" (Book 5.) But gradually, for social dancing, musicality becomes easier and easier, until you no longer have to think about it.

For this to work, there's a catch.

There are two factors which determine how well we do something:

- How simple it is

- How often we do it

When it comes to successfully completing tasks, humans are best at the simple things we do regularly. Unfortunately, we're also terrible at those complex tasks that we rarely encounter.

Fast Food joints are the epitome of this. If you order something standard, say a Large Big Mac Meal with Coke, the staff will probably get it right. It ticks the two boxes; it's simple and frequent - they fill that order a lot each day.

Order something more complicated and, like Leo, you're probably not going to end up with what you wanted. It's complicated and they rarely do that order. Because of that, the odds they'll get it right, just plummeted and you may well end up with tuna instead.

For social dancing, this means you want to be using the same, simple grammar of musicality all the time. By applying it to everything you dance, you'll tick *simple* and *often* and so can consistently get it right.

Choreography

"The important things are always simple; the simple are always hard. The easy way is always mined." ~ *Murphy*

Choreography involves complicated things, often ones that'll you'll rarely do. So why aren't performances filled with mistakes?

With choreography, you can simplify the problem enough to get away with inverted habeneras, by only having to remember them in specific places for that one performance and partner. Doing so simplifies things, a lot like having one person in the kitchen who's only in charge of the fries.

You can also rehearse the same choreography over and over in a short period of time; this effectively lets you tick *often*, though only for a limited period. Try it again a year later and most likely, it'll be full of mistakes.

Advanced Fundamentals

There's a trap of thinking that *simple* means *beginners* and that *complex* means *advanced*.

Where many social dancers go wrong, is they start climbing the choreography musicality mountain, rather than the social dancing musicality mountain. After they've learned what the beat is, they focus on learning complex ideas that they rarely get to use – ideal for choreography, but not so great for social dancing.

The more you try to take your social dancing musicality above a certain level of complexity and focus on things you rarely hear in the music, the more it will start to fail on you.

Rather than learning the simple grammar and then letting it become something they can do without thinking, those climbing 'Mount Choreography' and trying to use it socially, turn musicality into increasingly complex algebra, juggling equations in their heads trying to make it all work.

If professionals need hours to create the choreography for a single song, what chance have you got of doing a decent job in three minutes, making it up as you go?

This is why if you try to use the choreography approach to musicality when you're dancing socially, you'll reach a certain point and then get stuck.

It's just too hard.

It can be camouflaged a bit, by swapping in new equally complicated pieces of musicality and throwing out some of the old, giving you the feeling that you're making progress. But ultimately, beyond a certain point, you're just taking one step forward and one step back, going nowhere fast.

Summary

- *Make sure you're climbing the right mountain*

- *Dancing a choreography involves thinking ahead*

- *Social dancing can be "in the moment"*

- *We're better at simple things we do often*

- *Trying to choreograph a social dance in real time, is far more difficult than having a month to choreograph a single dance*

Chapter 2 Musical Punctuation

"I long for exclamation marks! But I'm drowning in ellipses..."

~ Isaac Marion

Songs used in this chapter:
"Star to Fall" by Cabin Crew

As a child, I remember seeing adverts in the back of comics that offered to set your poetry to music for a few dollars. I wondered if they just used the same music for everyone? This was before the internet, so they probably wouldn't get found out if they did...

Argentine Tango took the opposite approach, setting new pieces of music to established poems. As such, although not all tango music has lyrics, those that do, usually follow a very similar structure to poetry. Even those that don't, tend to fit the same pattern, as they're still part of the same musical genre.

Terminology – Musical Genre

Music that belongs to recognizable group, or follows specific conventions, such as Jazz, Classical and Hip hop.

In the same way you can perform a poem you've never seen before, you can dance to unfamiliar music by recognizing and using the same pattern. You can also use it to better understand music you are familiar with.

The Witching Hour

Let's see how this works, using a classic scene from Shakespeare's Macbeth - the three Witches are busy brewing up trouble!

"Double, double toil and trouble;

Fire burn and cauldron bubble.

Cool it with a baboon's blood,

Then the charm is firm and good."

The first line has eight syllables, which fits neatly into a set of eight beats.

Dou - ble, dou - ble

toil and trou - ble

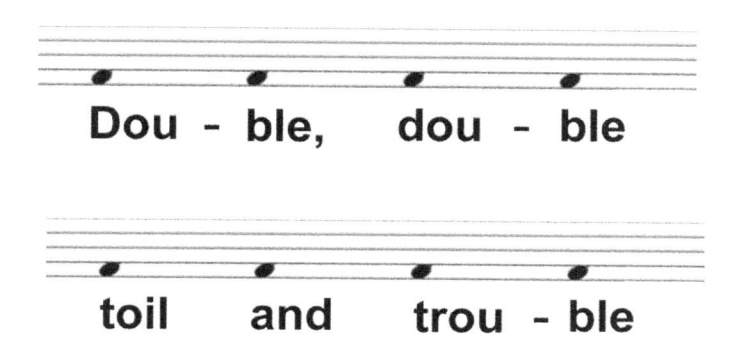

There are several places where you generally find musical punctuation in Argentine Tango music and these tend to be the same places you would find them in poetry:

Usually at the beginning, middle and end of specific words, lines and verses.

Terminology – Punctuation

Musical cues tend to come in predictable places

For example, if you were reading the Witches' speech, you'd probably start with a dramatic beginning, to let the audience know that something interesting is afoot!

Emphasis

To let you know where the musical cues are in the piece, musicians and singers often emphasize a specific part of the music – for example, a note, a word, or a series of notes.

One way you might emphasize the words to give the dancers musical cues would be like this,

"**One** two **three** four, **five** six **seven eight**,

One two three four five six seven eight.

One two three four, five six seven eight,

One two three four **five six seven eight**!"

Applying that to the witches, gives us,

*"**Double**, **double toil** and **trouble**;*

***Fire** burn and cauldron bubble.*

***Cool** it with a baboon's blood,*

***Then** the charm is **firm and good!**"*

It's not the only way you could choose to emphasize the words. Rather than finding the "best" way, what's more important at this stage is just whether it feels right?

For example, emphasizing it this way makes less sense.

*"Double, **double** toil and trouble;*

*Fire burn and caul**dron bub**ble.*

*Cool it with **a** baboon's blood,*

*Then **the** charm **is** firm **and** good!"*

Starting to find your way with the Musical Cues

Much as in poetry, the 'One' is often emphasized in the same way as the beginning of a sentence or verse. This helps to let the dancers know where they are in the music.

"**Double**, double..."

Because of this, The 'One' will usually have some sort of pause on the beat before it, shown with a ←.

"**Double,** double toil and trouble;←

Fire burn and cauldron bubble.←

Cool it with a baboon's blood,←

Then the charm is firm and good!←**"**

There's a hierarchy of musical cues. Verses are more important than lines, which in turn, are more important than words. The beginning and end, are also more significant than the middle.

This means that signaling the end of a verse to the dancers, is usually more important than a word in the middle of the verse.

Ideally, the more important the emphasis, the more warning the composer of the music will give you.

Here only "bubble" is emphasized, to let you know it's just the end of a sentence,

"*Fire burn and cauldron **bubble**.*"

Whereas, the end of the verse is usually more heavily emphasized, such as,

"Then the charm is firm and good!"

Another common way of placing the emphasis to warn of the ending a verse, is to begin just as you've just passed the mid-point of the last line,

*"Then the charm is ↓ **firm and good!**"*

As a dancer, this means when you've reached the last line of a verse, you know to be listening out for musical cues adding emphasis and alerting you to the upcoming end.

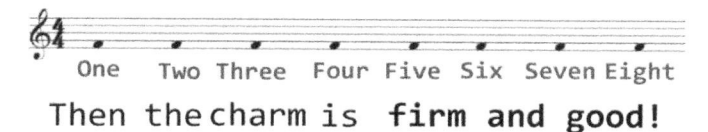

One　　Two　Three　Four　Five　Six　Seven　Eight
Then the charm is firm and good!

In turn, because you're expecting these musical cues, you'll be ready to react to them in your dancing as they arrive.

How Cues Punctuate the Music

Musicians punctuate their music in several ways. Pauses are often used in the same way as commas, periods and paragraph breaks. To emphasize a note, musicians will usually play it more loudly, or add a 'fill' of a few quick notes.

These cues are there to help you navigate your way through the piece. As with reading poetry, the emphasis tends to become more pronounced as you go from commas, to periods, to exclamation marks, reflecting their increasing importance in the music.

Recognizing the meaning of the cues lets you know where you are in the music.

Likewise, by knowing where you are, you have a

good idea of what cues are probably coming up so you can react to them in your dancing.

This is why being able to recognize the 'One' is such a good starting place. It's likely to have a strong emphasis that musically matches the feeling of starting a step or pivot. It also happens many times in each song, always in the same places, ticking the boxes for *simple* and *frequent*.

This is one of the main reasons that not all music is created equally, when it comes to dancing socially. A piece may be perfectly pleasant to sit down and listen to over wine, or sufficiently tricksy to make for an interesting choreography. But be too vague or unpredictable in its use of musical cues for social dancing, making it feel awkward and uncomfortable.

Exercise 1

Listen to "Star to Fall" by Cabin Crew.

It's a fairly blatant "The 'One to Eight' phrasing is here" song.

It starts with,

"This is your cabin crew speaking, please prepare for take-off."

This is unusual in that there's no accompanying rhythm or melody to these lyrics. Though rare, you'll encounter this in some Argentine Tango music, such as Carlos Gardel's, "Silencio."

With songs like this, the easiest solution is to wait until the rhythm actually starts; though with longer introductions of this kind, some dancers will get bored and start dancing to the internal rhythm in their head. Just remember to change back to the actual rhythm when it finally kicks in!

An elegant solution is to subtly start to move your foot during the lyrics / melody – such as a small circle, or slowly lifting the heel - and then complete the step as the Compás begins.

Feeling the Phrases

Fortunately, a set of eight beats in tango music is usually going to take about four seconds. If you can find the 'One', then you'll know where the 'Eight' is. Likewise the 'One' is immediately after the 'Eight', so finding the 'Eight' tells you where the 'One' is. And so on. Given that the 'One' and the 'Eight' tend to have emphasis, and often there's a pause between them, they're a useful tool to quickly find your place in the music.

Exercise 2

Listen to "Star to Fall" by Cabin Crew

After the intro, "Star to Fall" continues at five seconds with,

"Trying to catch you heart is like,

trying to catch your heart is like."

Listen to the faster drumbeat that kicks in halfway through the second line, warning you that the end of the line is approaching.

It's the musical equivalent of adding this emphasis

"Trying to catch you heart is like,

*trying to catch **your heart is like.**"*

The music builds on this and the next

"Trying to catch your heart is like,"

now has a thudding drumbeat running through it.

Musically we might consider it as,

*"**Trying to catch your heart is like**"*

What's particularly useful about this is that each "Trying" is on a 'One' and each "Trying to catch your heart is like" has eight beats. This makes it very helpful for practicing listening to the musical cues. It also gives you easy references in the lyrics to help you find the 'One' if you get lost. (Yes, it's really just going to repeat the same line over and over for the entire song.)

As you listen to the song, concentrate on recognizing the cues and use them to navigate where you are in the music. Keep practicing until you can comfortably recognize where the 'One', and 'Eight' are, as well as tell the difference between the end of a sentence and the end of a verse by the intensity of the emphasis used.

Troubleshooting

The accompanying official music video for this is probably not the best thing to put on if you're at work. It's not outright offensive, but it might raise eyebrows.

Summary

- *Musical punctuation in Argentine Tango tends to be the same as you would find in poetry*
- *It's usually at the beginning, middle and end of specific words, lines and verses.*
- *Musicians and singers often emphasize a specific part of the music – for example, a note, a word, or a series of notes*
- *The 'One' is often emphasized in the same way of the beginning of a sentence or verse*
- *Verses are usually more important than lines, which in turn, are more important than words*
- *The beginning and end are normally more significant than the middle*
- *Pauses are often used, effectively functioning the same as commas, periods and paragraph breaks*
- *To emphasize a note, musicians will usually play it more loudly, or add a 'fill' of 3 or 4 quick notes*
- *Sometimes there's no accompanying rhythm or melody to the lyrics*

- *Not all music is created equally*

Chapter 3 Rhythmic Punctuation

"Randomly throwing in triple steps as you dance another style, does not suddenly make it West Coast Swing!" ~ *Me, being grumpy.*

Used in this chapter:

<u>Songs</u>

"5, 6, 7, 8" by Steps

"Son of Man" by Phil Collins

"Make Me Smile" by Steve Harley

<u>Videos</u>

"Steps - 5, 6, 7, 8 (Official Video)" posted by StepsOfficial

"Sesame Street: Feist sings 1,2,3,4" posted by Sesame Street

One of the major differences between Argentine Tango and dance styles that focus on pop music, is that tango dancers actually make use of all the rhythms. Many social dances ignore the complex rhythms in pop music entirely, despite all the effort drummers put into them. Fortunately for us, they provide us with clear examples to practice with.

Exercise 3

Search Youtube for "Steps - 5, 6, 7, 8 (Official Video)" posted by StepsOfficial.

Skip ahead to 34 seconds to hear a 'fill' of drumbeats that they discretely ignore while running across a beach.

They then go into the dance routine; it seems like the drummer is behaving himself... only he's not. Listen carefully around 38 seconds and you'll hear them sneak in an extra beat. The dancers ignore it. There's another one at 52 - they ignore that too.

This happens to varying degrees in pop music. Most dance styles simply dance along to the Compás, ignoring these variations in rhythm. Tango dancers can choose to do the same, but also have plenty of tools for dancing these subtle extra beats (Books 5 and 6.)

Fortunately, as we've seen, the interesting bits usually come in certain places. They're often used as the musical punctuation for a song — commas, exclamation marks and so on.

Exercise 4

Listen to "Son of Man" by Phil Collins.

This song has helpful examples of using the drumbeat to emphasize the 'One' at the beginning of verses.

At the beginning, the first thing you'll notice is that as the lyrics begin with

"Huh!"

Phil briefly adds a quick 'fill' of four beats, emphasizing the beginning of the verse, before settling down for a bit. There's another drumbeat 'fill', just before

"Oh the power..."

as a heads-up to the listener that the next verse is about to begin.

Phil adds 'fills' in again at the end of

"will come to you in time."

as well as

"will reach the peak."

and at

"you will journey from boy to man."

Each time he's signaling the end of a sentence or verse.

The 'Five'

The 'Five' is also used, for the middle of a line, but tends to be briefer and more subtle, usually the equivalent of emphasizing after a comma. If you think of the verse as a paragraph, or a four-line poem, it might look like this,

*"One two three four, **five** six seven eight,*

*One two three four **five** six seven eight.*

*One two three four **five** six seven eight,*

*One two three four, **five** six seven eight!"*

Applying that to Shakespeare, we get,

*"Double double, **toil** and trouble,*

*Fire burn and **caul**dron bubble.*

*Cool it with a **bab**oon's blood,*

*Then the charm, **is firm** and good!"*

Just by making those small changes, it now has a different rhythm to it.

Exercise 5

Search Youtube for "Sesame Street: Feist sings 1,2,3,4", posted by Sesame Street.

Here every time she sings

"One, two, three, four"

is helpfully on the corresponding 'One, two, three, four' in the music. Use this to practice finding the 'Five' immediately after.

The End of a Verse

For the commas, the drummer might add a single extra beat, or pause. For the periods, a brief flurry of beats or longer pause. And for the exclamation mark they might go wild or have a much longer pause! Ideally the end of a verse has cues warning you. Exactly how obvious they are, varies from piece to piece.

Exercise 6

Listen to "Make Me Smile " by Steve Harley.

Steve Harley elevates the long pause after the end of a verse - also known as a 'break' - to an art form h with pauses at the end of his choruses you can Mack Truck through.

The chorus ends with

"I'll do what you want, running wild"

at 57 seconds, followed by four whole seconds of complete silence! This happens repeatedly throughout the song.

For now, practice stopping on the 'break.'

Troubleshooting

While it's a lot shorter, The Dixie Chicks' song "Goodbye Earl" has a break at 3 minutes and 10 seconds, which is helpfully announced by the lyrics,

"We need a break!"

There's a drumbeat 'fill' and then everyone freezes in a dramatic pose for a moment, as the music pauses. You can find it by searching Youtube for "Dixie Chicks - Goodbye Earl (Official Video)", posted by dixiechicks

Sharp Turn Ahead!

These extra beats, notes and pauses are there to help you navigate your way through the music. The longer 'fills' tend to start ahead of time, giving you warning that the 'Eight' is coming up, especially at the end of a sentence or verse.

Statement of the 'Obvious' 1

By knowing where the cues tend to punctuate music, you can reliably navigate by them, rather than having to memorize songs, or do math as you dance.

Just check for cues as you approach the punctuation points.

Exercise 7

Search Youtube for "Steps - 5, 6, 7, 8 (Official Video)" posted by StepsOfficial.

During the intro, the drum-beat kicks in on the 'Five', continuing all the way through to the 'Eight' before the women start singing. A similar thing happens with a flurry of beats at 1 minute and 42 seconds. Both act as a way of saying,

"Pay attention!"

There's a Big Ending
Get ready!

Big One
Next

This makes a lot more sense with Spanish punctuation which alerts you to emphasis sooner. In English, if you read out loud

"Woo-hoo!"

you're supposed to emphasize the entire word. But the exclamation mark only tells you this after you've read to the end of the word.

In Spanish, you get an early warning with,

"¡Woo-hoo!"

With a bit of artistic license, you could think of the drumbeat in Steps as,

"One two three four

¡Five six seven eight!"

A similar method in English, is to use bold text,

"One two three four

five six seven eight!"

Don't Miss Your Exit

"Turn left here." ~ Anna, 'giving directions' just as we passed the exit.

After a flurry of beats has finished, the next beat is usually the 'One.'

Good music also has some extra clues to help you out; the 'Five' often gives you an extra cue, and may be further supported by the 'Seven' to show that this 'Eight' is really important!

Think of it like the "Next Exit" sign on the Interstate. If you miss your exit, it's a big deal. So you get an extra couple of signs ahead of the actual turn-off to warn you. This also gives you time to do anything important. On an Interstate you might want to change lanes; in a tango song, you might want to be in a comfortable position to allow your partner to adorn the upcoming pause.

If you've lost where you are in the song, but then hear those cues, you now have a good idea that if the musicians are making this much fuss, you're probably near the end of a verse, or even the song.

Synergies

At other times, the 'Five' just sits back and chills, leaving it to the 'Seven' to warn you.

Generally, the more pronounced the 'Seven', the more important the 'Eight' is. Likewise, the emphasis on the 'Eight' is hopefully proportional to the importance of the next 'One.' The synergy between them helps you navigate. A little fuss is more likely signaling the end of a sentence or phrase,

"Five, six, seven, **eight**"

But lots of fuss is usually warning you that the verse about to end,

"Five, six, **SEVEN, EIGHT!**"

In the Steps song "5, 6, 7, 8", the lyrics start at the beginning of the song (7 seconds.) Musically, this is important, so you get a warning with the drumbeat cue, running all the way through the 'Five', 'Six', 'Seven' and 'Eight' (5 to 7 seconds) to really make sure you know it's about to happen.

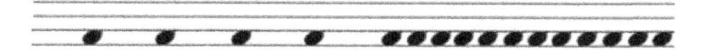

Get ready, something's coming up!

They even go a step further, by actually saying

"It's time to begin, now count it in, five, six, seven, eight!"

in order to remove any trace of doubt.

I Don't Think We're in Kansas any More...

"We'll get the next (ending)!" ~ *various followers*

The compliment is most often receive about my musicality is that I "really feel the music." I've reached the point where I just feel the cues and respond, rather than having to actually think about what I'm doing.

One of the benefits of getting comfortable with the structure of social musicality, is that if the DJ has chosen a weird piece of music, or if you're dancing to live music and the band is feeling playful, you and your partner will probably make the same 'mistakes.'

If the music ends abruptly on a 'Seven' rather than an 'Eight', because the DJ's laptop accidentally cut out the last second of the song, you may both step on a note that isn't there, because you feel there should have been another note.

Or you may both stop on the 'Eight' at the end of the song; but then the band decides to throw in a few extra notes...

When this happens, there's a few things to bear in mind. If the band is being playful, they'll hopefully pay attention to the dancers and adjust themselves accordingly. There's a fine line between 'playful' and 'irritating.'

Whatever happened, remember this isn't ballroom dancing. It's not a competition, no-one's marking you down.

However, I've consistently found the opposite happens; by admitting that you felt the music should have done something else, especially when you partner clearly felt the same, you create camaraderie rather than embarrassment.

Summary

- *In tango, you can dance to all the rhythms that you hear in the music*

- *The 'Five' can be emphasized, but tends to be briefer and more subtle, usually the equivalent of the word after a comma*

- *Ideally, the end of a verse has cues warning you as it approaches*

- *Extra beats, notes and pauses are deliberately put throughout the music, to help you navigate your way*

- *If you've lost where you are in the song, listen out for cues to get back on track*

- *The longer 'fills' tend to start ahead of time, giving you warning that the 'Eight' is coming up, especially at the end of a sentence or verse.*

- *Generally, the more pronounced the 'Seven', the more important the 'Eight' is. Likewise, the emphasis on the 'Eight' is hopefully proportional to the importance of the next 'One'*

- ***It's not a competition, no-one's marking you down.***

Chapter 4 La Cumparsita

> *"If you realized,*
> *that still inside my soul,*
> *I uphold that affection*
> *I had for you..."* ~ *La Cumparsita*

Used in this chapter:

Videos

"Tango Orchestra Club Atlanta: La Cumparsita" posted by Clint Rauscher

In pop music, if at any point in the song you want to find the Compás, then you listen to the drums. There may some pauses or "messing around", but for almost all the time, the drums are your go-to instrument.

In tango, things can be a lot more fluid. Any of the instruments can play the Compás and they can also pass it around between them, as if playing American Football.

"End of the tanda. Fourteen seconds left, the bandoneon takes the snap and has the Compás, He's looking for the piano... he throws deep to the left, the

piano's caught it at the Eight. Only five seconds left...But now he's going down... Oh, look at this! The violins! The violins have the Compás. **Touchdooooown!** *What an ending. You've gotta be kidding me! The improvisation of the musicians was incredible.'*

La Cumparsita: Part 1

La Cumparsita has some nice rhythmic qualities, particularly a Compás that's good for walking and cuddle-shuffling (Book 3.) However, compared with songs like Poema, this is going to be a lot dirtier, as the musicians play fast and loose with the rhythm.

Exercise 8

Search for "Tango Orchestra Club Atlanta: La Cumparsita" posted by Clint Rauscher.

This version of La Cumparsita is a good piece with which to explore how the instrument marking the Compás changes as the piece progresses. It's around the 120 BMP mark – a nice, comfortable two claps per second – great for social tango.

Watch it through once. Don't panic. We'll deal with it

one piece at a time.

Go back to the beginning. The opening shot is of two bandoneon players. The older one of the left is the trouble-maker, so for now, focus on the younger one to the right. See how he's bouncing the bandoneon along to the beat.

To start with, they're both behaving and keep to the *thud-thud* beat until the first pause at 16 seconds. If you keep clapping, you see they come back in "on time" at 19 seconds.

However, at 22 seconds, the older player gets bored and starts doing *other stuff* - so stay with the player on the right. There's another pause at 34 seconds. Let's stop there for now.

The Vanishing Compás

The Compás is going to move around between the instruments a lot in this song as well as fading in and out. If you're struggling, both with this piece and tango music in general, know that you're listening for something that's basically going at two beats per second. It won't be far off that. If there's nothing obvious, try something consistently doing one beat per second.

Once you find it, with practice, you can adjust your own internal rhythm to match it. Now, even if the music pauses, or the beat gets too quiet to hear, you still know roughly where it is.

It's important to know there are limits to how long you can accurately keep a rhythm going internally without hearing it. There's a game where a well-known piece of pop music is played for about twenty seconds, then the volume is muted. The people playing sing for about ten seconds and the volume is then brought back to normal, to see how closely they now match it. Usually, they've already gotten significantly out of time with the music.

Fortunately, good composers know this and won't leave dancers guessing for too long. But be prepared to adjust, once you can hear the Compás again.

La Cumparsita: Part 2

The music restarts at 35 seconds and our loyal bandoneonist on the right is still pumping out the beat. When the camera pulls back, if you watch his foot, you can see his heel keeping time.

Another pause. Now the violins join in, making it much harder to hear the bandoneon.

This happens a lot in tango for a variety of reasons.

For this piece, you've had almost a minute to tune into the Compás. In jazz and blues music, this is often the moment in the song when each musician will get a moment to do a solo and show-off their *Mad Skillz*.

In tango, it's more like shining a spot-light on one kind of instrument at a time. The other instruments either quieten down, or stop doing interesting things, so that your attention is drawn to the one that's front and center.

Right now, that's the violins going,

"Look at me!"

At 57 seconds, the camera zooms in as the musical spotlight moves onto the bandoneons — we can see that now they're both playing around. However, the younger player quickly goes back to playing the Compás. It's an important job and he can't abandon it for too long, without risking losing the dancers.

If you've ever done a keep-fit class you'll recognize this effect. As long as the teacher is either moving to the beat, or at least calling out the beat in some way -

even if it's as simple as "1, 2, 3, 4" - everything's fine. But if they get distracted by someone coming in and asking for directions to another class, it's surprising just how quickly everyone starts to lose the beat and move out of sync with each-other.

At 1 minute and 4 seconds something interesting happens and fortunately the cameraman zooms in on it. The violinists start playing the Compás! Look closely at how they play and you'll see all their strokes are short and downwards to help create this choppy, rhythmic effect.

To re-cap, so far:

- The two bandoneonists start off playing the Compás

- The one on the right pretty much stays on it 95% of the time, though he does pause with the rest of the musicians.

- How easy it is to hear the bandoneons varies as other instruments are given the spot-light

- The bandoneon is not the only instrument to

mark the beat. The violins join in too when the bandoneon is given the spotlight

La Cumparsita: Part 3

Now, let's skip ahead to the perfect storm at 3 minutes and 6 seconds. Here the piano is playing the melody. Meanwhile, both bandoneons, the violinists and the double bassists are playing the rhythm. There's a pause at 3 minutes and 10 seconds, but this goes on for a while.

From 3 minutes and 30 seconds the violinist on the left starts their moment in the spotlight.

The pianist helps support the violins by playing the Compás with her right hand. Yes, the specific piano keys / notes change, but her hand is still doing a steady *thud-thud-thud* up-and-down motion.

Compared to most pop music, that's a lot more complicated. Each of the four instruments has taken a turn, both in playing the Compás as well as doing *other things*. For the spotlight moments in this song, the rest of the instruments shift to playing the Compás.

Compare all of that, with pop music where the rhythm is usually thought of as

"It's the drum."

Summary

- *Any of the instruments can play the Compás and they can also pass it around between them*

- *If you're struggling to find the Compás, listen for a rhythm that's about 2 beats per second*

- *You can use your own internal rhythm keep track of it if the music pauses, or the beat gets too quiet to hear*

- *Often one instrument will be given the 'spotlight.'*

- *This can move from one instrument to another throughout the piece*

Chapter 5 Melody

> *"It was a dream of sweet love,*
> *hours of happiness and loving,*
> *it was the poem of yesterday "*
> ~ Poema

Songs used in this chapter:

"Overdrive" by Lazerhawk

"Bahia Blanca" by Carlos DiSarli

"Star to Fall" by Cabin Crew

"Son of Man" by Phil Collins

"Poema" by Francisco Canaro

Videos

"El Muro - Bahía Blanca - Live at Cosmopolite" posted by El Muro Tango

"Orianthi - According To You (Official Video)" posted by OfficialOrianthi.

"javier y geraldine bailan poema" posted by Silvia Tangueira

In Argentine Tango, the line between rhythm and

melody often gets blurred. Quite simply, in pop music, a drum can't play a melody. But, in tango, musicians can move between playing the rhythm and the melody by varying how percussively their instruments are used.

As we've seen, certain notes and words can be emphasized to give the dancers cues as to where they are in the song and what's about to happen. With lyrics and melody, the options expand:

- Getting louder or softer
- Singing a word of the lyrics, or playing a note, higher or deeper
- Lengthening or shortening the time to sing the word, or play a note.

With a single drum, you can only really do the first option. The second is doable, but needs another drum. For the third, the best you can do are 'fills', by playing a quick succession of notes, separate from the Compás.

Tango has a bit more wiggle room. When the instruments play the rhythm, they can also play a higher or deeper note. They can also play a longer one; but then you get into the issue of at which point is it long enough that they've changed from rhythm to melody?

'Fills' are a safer option, but raise the question,

"If a tango instrument plays a 'fill' using notes, is it a rhythm, or a melody?"

Extending this idea, if you play a tune to the Compás, is that the rhythm or the melody? Or both?

Exercise 9

Listen to "Overdrive" by Lazerhawk.

This starts off with a steady, fast drumbeat - the Compás. It's accompanied by rhythmic notes from the synthesizer, so if the drumbeat was muted, you'd still be able to make a good guess at the Compás.

At 2 minutes and 3 seconds, everything changes. The drumbeat slows and the notes become far more melodic. They vary considerably in length - now if the drumbeat was muted, you wouldn't be able to guess what the Compás was.

With that in mind, let's look at a piece of Argentine Tango music that's very melody driven.

Exercise 10

Search for "El Muro - Bahía Blanca - Live at Cosmopolite" posted by El Muro Tango on Youtube.

For now, we're only interested in what the first 30

seconds tell us.

It starts with 14 seconds of piano.

And no rhythm.

At all.

This tells us we're going to need to pay attention to the piano during this piece and the rhythm is going to be elusive. Well, that's a problem, especially if you want to dance on the Compás.

The double-bassist eventually joins in with a handful of rhythmic notes, which at least match the standard Compás speed of 'two per second' you're listening out for, so now we know we've found the Compás as well as its actual speed.

Then the double-bassist abandons us and starts a duet with the violinist! Will the bandoneonist save us?

Apparently not.

So to recap, we currently know:

- The Compás
- Hearing the rhythm is going to be problematic
- All the instruments are going to go off and do interesting things, instead of being helpful
- The music is written so that your attention will gradually move between the different

instruments - the 'spotlight' approach

In short, this would be a terrible song if you were just starting to learn how to find the beat.

Exercise 11

Search for "Alma de Tango White Party 2012, Improvisation to Bahia Blanca" posted by Monica Llobet. (Richard Council also posted the same duplicate video.)

Watch the first 40 seconds.

These are professional dancers who know what they're doing - that's a perfectly good, musical interpretation of Bahia Blanca. But did you have any real sense of the Compás? Either in the music itself, or by watching them?

Probably not.

So how do we deal with Bahia Blanca's elusive Compás? There's two schools of thought. One solves the problem with,

"You can step on any note as long as there's an accompanying beat from the Compás."

As long as the bandoneon is thumping away, then

you could dance on any of the violin notes (gray) which match the Compás (black).

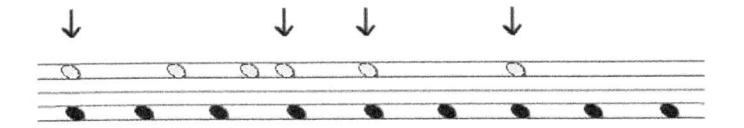

↓   ↓ ↓   ↓

Unfortunately, this isn't going to work here, as the lack of underlying rhythm means you'd be stuck for large portions of this song without a matching Compás.

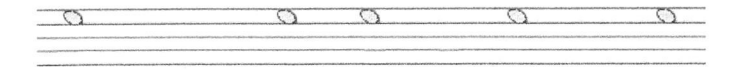

The other approach simply says,

"You can step on any note."

Ok, much better. With this, you can step on the violin notes in Bahia Blanca, despite the silent Compás.

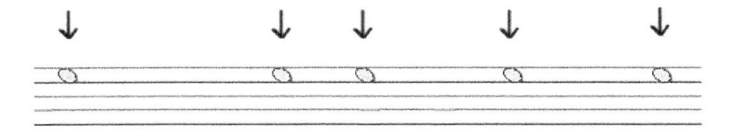

↓   ↓ ↓   ↓   ↓

This usually produces a very different feel - melodic rather than rhythmic. There's still a relationship between them, but melodic dancing tends to be looser.

It's a t-shirt and jeans, to rhythmic's pressed suit and trousers.

It's notable that neither of these solutions actually tries to draw a line between when a note is part of a rhythm or a melody. They're not concerned with how long a note lasts. The first just cares whether it's on the Compás, The second is only concerned that a note is played – no stepping when there's silence, or adding in *tac tac tac* steps when there's no accompanying notes!

In Argentine Tango the length of the note is mainly reflected in your dancing by your choice of Dinámica – usually staccato for short, rhythmic notes and legato for longer ones (Book 6.)

But how do you know which notes to step on?

Should you step on all the notes that you're "allowed" to, or just some of them? We come back to the different way that some notes will be more pronounced than others.

Exercise 12

Search for "Alma de Tango White Party 2012, Improvisation to Bahia Blanca" posted by Monica

Llobet. (Richard Council also posted the same duplicate video.)

Jump ahead to 30 seconds. Watch all the way up to a minute; notice how each step they make is on a note that's more emphasized.

Levels of Emphasis

The odd beats - 'One', 'Three', 'Five' and 'Seven' - are usually going to be slightly more emphasized than the even ones – 'Two', 'Four', 'Six' and 'Eight' - to show the Compás.

Extra emphasis is then added on top of this pattern to add further musical cues.

"**One**, two, **three**, four, **five**, six, **seven**, eight."
Might become,
"**One**, two, **three**, four, **five**, six, **seven**, **eight**."
Or even,
"**One**, two, **three**, four, **five**, **six**, Seven, **EIGHT!**"
The added emphasis may also be done with the melody or lyrics (shown in gray), such as,
"**One**, two, **three**, four, **five**, six, **seven**, eight."

Or,

"**One**, two, **three**, four, **five**, six, Seven, EIGHT!"

Fortunately the lyrics and melody also follow the same basic punctuation as rhythm when they want to add emphasis; the interesting bits usually come in certain places, often used as the musical punctuation for a song – commas, exclamation marks and so on – and are often accompanied with addition musical cues, letting you know where you are in the song and if anything important is coming up.

'Rises'

As we've already seen, both here and in Book 5, the music can also 'rise' and build, adding increasing emphasis to warn you of something coming up ahead.

The speed of the 'rise' can also tell how fast this particular *something* is approaching. A nice gentle 'rise', signals to you when there's a good stretch of road ahead. You can relax and dance, without having to worry about pauses for a while. Whereas a sudden change warns you that something important is almost on top of you.

Exercise 13

Listen to "Star to Fall" by Cabin Crew.

The continual 'rise' in emphasis from 'One' to 'Three' lets you know there probably isn't going to be a pause on the 'Four', so if you want to step or adorn all the beats in your dancing, you can. The continuation of the

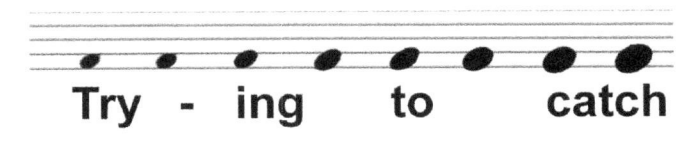

Try - ing   to   catch

'rise' from 'Four' to 'Eight' reinforces this.

Exercise 14

Watch "Orianthi - According To You (Official Video)" posted on Youtube by OfficialOrianthi.

It starts with two single notes.

Then there's singing and some guitar up to 10 seconds. However both the lyrics and the guitar are deliberately bland - there's no real emphasis being placed on the notes or words, yet.

A drumbeat joins in and carries through to 18

seconds. But again, it's just a basic beat, nothing particularly *artistic*.

A more interesting guitar melody begins, which lasts through to 28 seconds.

Then the guitar goes wild for a few seconds!

There's a pause...

And then everything kicks in – the drums start doing artistic things, both the guitar melody and the lyrics now have lots of emphasis.

It's notable that up to that first pause, everyone is largely static. Orianthi is either sitting, or standing, but not doing much. Whereas when everything finally kicks in, you see people in the background start to get up and dance around and the musicians are now moving a lot more.

This is a great example of the music building, layer by layer to a climax:

- ✔ Bland lyrics and melody
- ✔ Calm Compás
- ✔ More interesting melody
- ✔ Melodic 'fill'
- ✔ Pause
- ✔ GO WILD!

As a dancer, you get a nice, clear set of signs telling you that the music is building and building. The guitar only going wild for a few seconds, combined with the Pause is there to say,

"Ok, annnnd NOW!"

Let's look at how Son of Man uses this idea more subtly.

Exercise 15

Listen to "Son of Man" by Phil Collins.

Jump ahead to 1 minute and 1 second. Feel the music just coasting along, until at about 1 minute and 7 seconds, when it starts to 'rise', letting you know the singer is soon going to come back in on the 'One.'

The melody then just trots along calmly. It's a basic "dum-da-dum" all the way through to 1.35 when again it builds to let you know the end of the phrase is coming up with,

"a man in time you'll be."

From 1.32 to 1.37 there's a brief flurried xylophone section, heralding the return of the singer with the lyrics,

"In learning you will teach,"

Each time, the music gives you a heads-up that the end of an important phrase is coming and the beginning of a new phrase is about to happen.

Let's look at an example of this in tango.

Exercise 16

Listen to first 35 seconds of "Poema" by Francisco Canaro.

The beginning has a nice, gentle melody that repeats itself. It's just wandering over and saying,

"Hi."

There's a calm piano 'fill' at the end of each phrase to act as punctuation and let you know where you are. It's reassuring you that everything's fine.

At 19 seconds, the music becomes a bit more pronounced. The notes are higher than before and now the piano adds in twice as many notes. Instead of the piano 'fill' at the end of the phrase, we get a bold bandoneon telling us that a new – quite possibly different - phrase is about to start.

Provided you like rhythmic music, Canaro's Poema is great to dance socially. It has a clear Compás and a clean structure that gives you ample cues of where you are, so you can just dance, without worrying about being suddenly caught out. Yet there's still enough going on to keep you interested. Unlike, say most of Biagi's tangos, Canaro's Poema isn't obnoxious. It invites you to use the musicality options (Book 6) provided by the lyrics, rhythm and melody, but at no point does it force you to.

You'll always have the safe option of staying with the Compás.

Exercise 17

Search Youtube for "javier y geraldine bailan poema" posted by Silvia Tangueira.

This is a great example of switching back and forth between dancing to Poema's strong Compás, eg from 20 to 38 seconds, and dancing to the melody, eg from 38 to one minute.

Summary

- *Musicians can move between playing the rhythm and the melody by varying how percussively their instruments are used*
- *They can add emphasis in many ways*
- *Getting louder or softer*
- *Singing a word of the lyrics, or playing a note, higher or deeper*
- *Lengthening or shortening the time to sing the word, or play a note*
- *In some tangos, hearing the Compás is a problem*
- *"You can step on any note as long as there's an accompanying beat from the Compás"*
- *"You can step on any note"*
- *The lyrics and melody also follow the same basic punctuation as rhythm when they want to add emphasis*
- *Music can also 'rise' and build, adding emphasis to warn you of something coming up ahead*
- *The speed of the 'rise' can also tell how fast this*

particular something is approaching

- *Ideally, the music gives cues to warn you that the end of an important phrase is coming and the beginning of a new phrase is about to happen*
- *With some music You'll always have the safe option of staying with the Compás*
- *It's perfectly acceptable to switch between dancing to the rhythm, melody and lyrics, depending on which you and your partner prefer and what's most dominant in the music at the time*

Chapter 6 Lyrics and Poetry

"I've got words in my head, so I sing them." ~ *Boogie Pimps*

Used in the chapter:

Songs

"Son of Man" by Phil Collins

"Poema" by Francisco Canaro

Bahia Blanca by Carlos DiSarli

Videos

"Maud Pie: Gneiss Work (Feat. Gina M.)" posted by ABagOfVicodin

"Nuevo Tango Performance" posted by Salsoul Dance School(Gangnam)

"Elena Velasco y Luis Rodriguez tango 1" posted by Satretango

To better understand how the melody uses the various punctuation points, it helps to look at the lyrics. The lyrics have actual punctuation and are generally written like poetry,

"Son of man, look to the sky.
Lift your spirit, set it free;
Some day you'll walk tall with pride,
Son of man, a man in time you'll be."

We naturally hear the punctuation. It's exactly the same as someone reciting a poem. With a skilled reader, they'll use their voice to emphasize different parts of it; in particular, the ending of sentences and verses.

Statement of the 'Obvious' 2

"To emphasize something, just do it in a different way to everything else."

There's quite a few ways for the singer to accomplish this using the same methods as musicians for emphasizing parts of the melody:

- The Compás
- Getting louder or softer
- Getting higher or deeper
- Lengthening or shortening the time it takes to

sing a word

Statement of the 'Obvious' 3

"To emphasize notes, you can do the same things you do with words"

Before we look at a specific example, let's look at what (hopefully) doesn't happen in either poetry or song; speaking, or singing, in a monotone.

Exercise 18

Search for "Maud Pie: Gneiss Work (Feat. Gina M.)" posted by ABagOfVicodin.

Youtube has a number of similar videos – just search for "speaking in a monotone" if this one's been taken down. However, I particularly like this one, because telling jokes in a monotone is so unnatural, you can instinctively feel where the emphasis should be.

Gina still uses punctuation. But the whole thing feels, wrong.

After you've watched it, search for "Maud Pie: Gneiss Work Bloopers!" and watch that. By comparison, when she breaks character, her voice is practically musical! Particularly from about half-way through, when she starts to get the giggles.

Exercise 19

Listen to "Son of Man" by Phil Collins.

At 1 minute and 53 seconds, you'll hear Phil's voice go down and become deeper on the "love" of,

"ones you **love.**"

This lets you know that although there's a pause, there's still more coming.

Whereas at the end of the verse at 2 minutes and 7 seconds, his voice gets both higher and louder, especially on "all", signaling the end of the verse,

"Well the time is drawing

near now, **it's yours to claim it ALL**!"

Troubleshooting

If you struggle with this exercise or the next, go back to listening to Maud's monotone for a bit, then try again.

Exercise 20

Listen to "Poema" by Francisco Canaro.

Listen to the lyrics which start at 52 seconds. The singer, Roberto Maida, extends the words to show you where the beginning and end of each phrase are, like this,

"<u>Cuaaaaan</u>-do las flores de tu ros-<u>aaaal</u>,

<u>Vuuuue</u>lv-an mas bellas a florec-<u>eer</u>,

<u>Reeeee</u>-cordarás mi quer-<u>eer</u>,

Y has de sab-<u>eer</u>,

Todo mi intenso <u>maaaa</u>-**AAAL!**"

You can hear the extra loudness at the end as well as the extension of "mal." to "*maaaa-**AAAL!***", to really let you know you've reached the end of the verse.

When the Compás is Missing in Action

Let's go back to DiSarli's Bahia Blanca and see how this works with the melody.

Exercise 21

Listen to "Bahia Blanca" by Carlos DiSarli

The beginning tells you that there's no real rhythm or Compás being marked by an instrument. However, there are emphasized notes where you'd expect the odd beats to be, so that's a clue as to where the Compás probably is.

There's a pause at the 'Four' and the 'Eight,' further confirming that the emphasized notes are sounding on the odd beats. These notes are about the right rhythm to fit with tango music, further confirming where the Compás is hiding.

There's also a 'fill' of notes to let you know when the 'Eight' is coming.

A safe approach to dancing this would be to walk confidently on the 'One' and the 'Three' and then collect and pause on the 'Four.' Walk again on the 'Five' and 'Seven' and pause for the 'fill' of notes at the 'Eight.'

You could adorn the 'fills', but the problem is you

need to know what they're going to be, in order to do it accurately. That's fine if you know the piece. Or if it's pretty repetitive, you might get a feel for what's coming later on.

But what about at the beginning when you're hearing it for the first time?

A more sophisticated way is to lead a pivot over the 'fill' at the 'Eight.' Think of it as *sweeping up the notes* in the 'fill' leading the pivot all the way into the next 'One.'

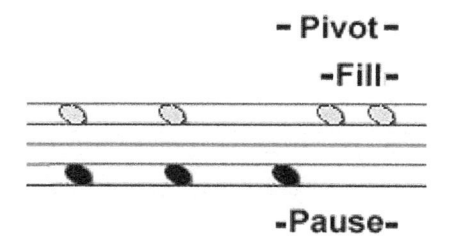

- Pivot -
-Fill-

-Pause-

The other thing to bear in mind is that your partner might know the piece. So for example, the leader may pause because he doesn't know whether the 'fill' will be two notes, or three. But if you're following and know it's two notes, you could do an adornment - such as tapping out both notes - in the space the leader gives you in that pause.

**Fill &
Taps
↓ ↓**

Pause

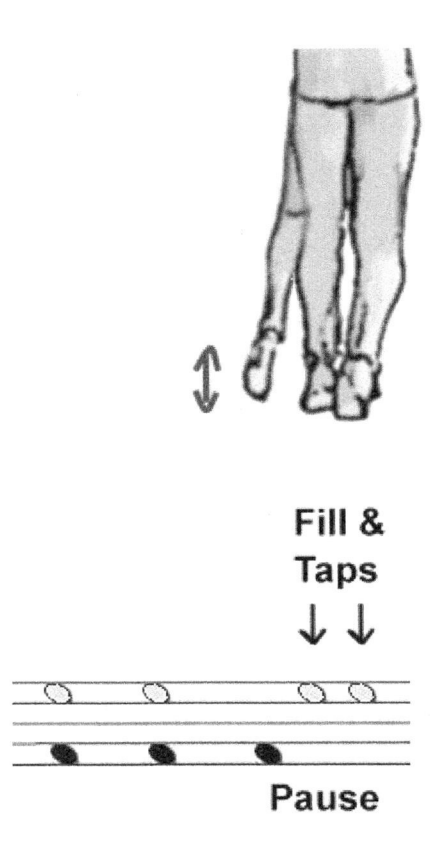

Similarly, if leader knows the piece well, and the follower doesn't, the leader could choose to adorn the notes by tapping their free foot.

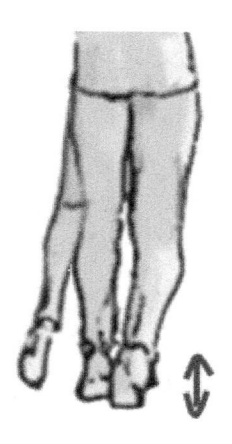

The other option, similar to pivoting, is making an small arc or circle with your free foot or leg, as an adornment over the same notes. Again, think of it as *sweeping up the notes* in the 'fill.' Again, this can be done by either, or both, partners.

— Arc —
-Fill-
-Pause-

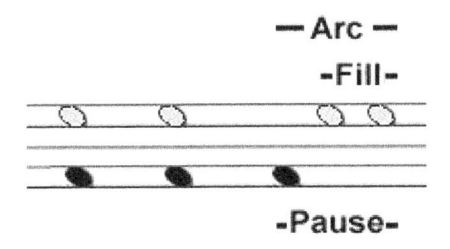

And that will get you safely through Bahia Blanca.

Exercise 22

Go through Bahia Blanca on your own, and using the pattern of:

- Step on the 'One' and 'Three'
- Collect on the 'Four'
- Step on the 'Five' and 'Seven'
- Pivot or adorn on the 'fills' after the 'Eight'

Breaking it down

Some teachers count beats as you go through a sequence. This is usually to try to keep everyone taking the same steps at the same time.

An offshoot of this, involves breaking down the beats into smaller parts for when there's additional steps going on between the beats, for example if you wanted to step on all the notes in a 'fill.'

"One, two" becomes "One-and-a-two", still said over the same two beats.

One　　Two

One Anda Two

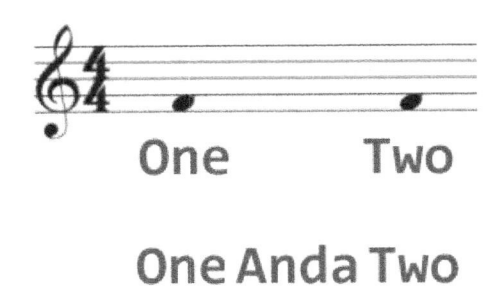

At this point, things are moving so quickly, it's largely irrelevant what exactly "and" and "a" mean in terms of time and fractions of seconds. Knowing there's two things that have to fit evenly in-between the beats is usually good enough.

Alternatively "tac" gets used in the same way to mean "fraction of a beat" such as,

"You step 'tac, tac, tac.'"

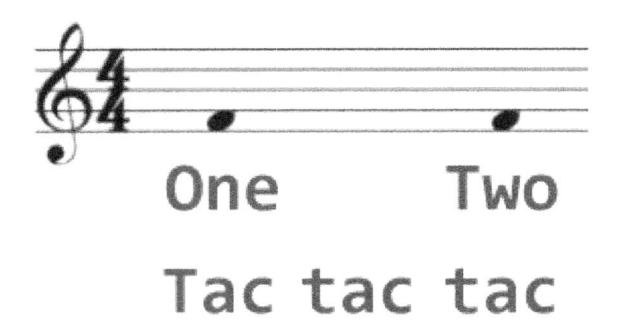

One　　Two

Tac tac tac

Again, the exact meaning varies – just to confuse things, some teachers will also use it for marking double-time.

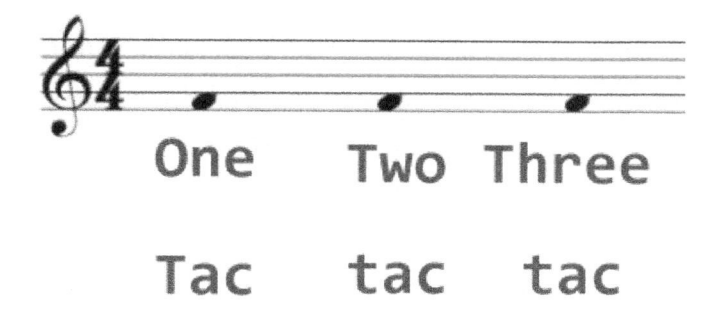

```
One    Two   Three
Tac    tac   tac
```

"You're not the Boss of Me!"

While the 'One' is important for navigating music, and getting practice finding and hearing it in class is valuable, it's also important to know that in social dancing, you're never actually obliged to start on it.

It's a balancing act - it's often easier to do so, as your partner is probably expecting that, making it smoother to lead and follow. So much so, in fact, that most people do. But if you've just missed it, in songs with longer phrasing, it can feel awkward waiting for the next 'One' to come around. In which case, it's often better to just start, rather than both of you feeling increasingly uneasy as you wait.

This also applies to when you "take a moment" to do movements to adorn your dancing and interpret the music, such as tapping out a 'fill.' It's easier to end your 'moment' - and the adornment - by stepping on the 'One' and continuing to dance. But again, with longer phrases, adorning for too long, can also get increasingly uncomfortable.

This is especially true if you accidentally just missed the 'One' after a short 'fill' and are now facing the prospect of adorning all the way around to the next 'One'; if it feels better to go ahead and step on a beat other than the 'One', rather than to wait, it's usually a good idea to do so.

Some dancers enjoy building this tension, rather than releasing it. With more experience, you'll get a feel for when, how long, and with whom, deliberately delaying until the next 'One' can be surprisingly enjoyable with.

Cruising

Now let's pay attention to the other cues that DiSarli

gives us in this piece.

At 34 seconds the melody begins. Until now, DiSarli has been using the punctuation to warn you of the many pauses in this section. But now he changes. There's no emphasis on this 'Three', letting you know that instead of pausing on the 'Four', you can just keep walking.

"Can" is important. If you choose to pause on this 'Three', it's not wrong.

Exercise 23

Listen to "Bahia Blanca" by Carlos DiSarli.

As it plays, either walk or pause. Listen to where the music suggests you can just cruise and where it's suggesting that you pause. Try out different variations. See what works. It's also useful to experiment with what doesn't work as well. Deliberately pause in the "wrong" places, or walk through the pauses.

The "Right" Way

Musicality is a lot like ordering a meal.

There's the basic meal. Say a burger and chips. That's the "Walk, pause, walk, pause" from Exercise 22.

You can choose to add sides or extras. Maybe you want bacon with your burger and some onion rings? So you add a pivot on the 'Eight' and you choose to keep walking through this 'Four.'

Maybe you want less? No tomatoes, please. So you get rid of the pause on all the 'Fours' and just walk through them.

Which is how you can have a room full of people all dancing differently to the same music. You can dance to the same music for years, each time varying it in some way.

Similarly I've used "walk" here for simplicity. But it's

really just any step over two beats. Likewise, there's nothing to stop you pivoting, instead of walking. Or stepping on every beat. Or syncopating with little tics and tacs. Ultimately all the tango "moves" are really just combinations of pivots, steps and collects, danced to different Dinámica and rhythms.

Almost by definition, it's difficult to find a video on Youtube of a plain burger version of "Bahia Blanca" - or any other tango song for that matter - that just uses walks and pivots. Understandably, most performances have all the toppings, which is fine, but unfortunately it also makes it harder to see what's going on.

Exercise 24

Search Youtube for "Nuevo Tango Performance" posted by Salsoul Dance School(Gangnam).

This is at the nuevo end of the spectrum.

When they're stepping, it's on the Compás, which helpfully has been enhanced in the audio of this version. While there's a lot of nuevo moves going on, they still make good use of pivoting over the gaps in the Compás.

Exercise 25

Search Youtube for "Elena Velasco y Luis Rodriguez tango 1" posted by Satretango.

Here are some elegant examples of how to use this idea to move through the pauses and 'fills.' Rather than pivoting, Luis simply leads Elena to slowly collect over the 'fills' at 17 and 25 seconds, accomplishing the same thing.

At 48 seconds there's a pivot over a 'fill' which Elena adorns.

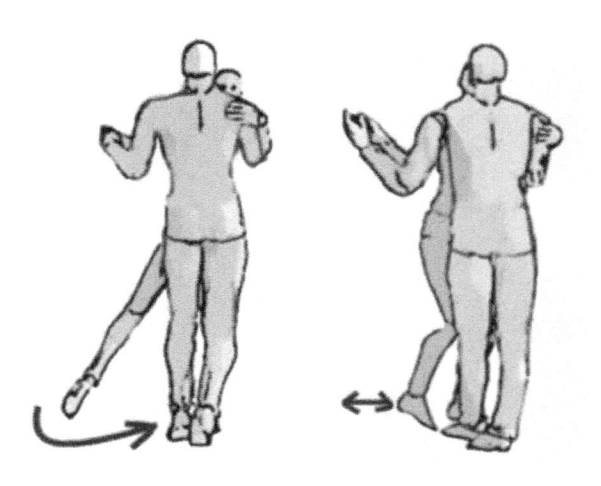

And at 1 min 14 there's a cheeky pivot to cause Elena to front boleo over the momentary pause in the lyrics and melody.

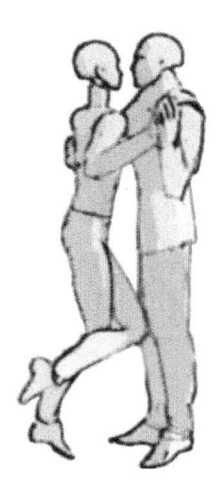

The video is a good compilation of musicality. At 33 seconds, Luis walks on the notes of the melody, rather than waiting for the bandoneon to restart the Compás.

Watch it through and see what else you can spot.

Summary

- *We naturally hear punctuation in poetry and conversation*
- *To emphasize something, do it in a different way to everything else*
- *Listening to someone talking in a monotone can help you tune in to the subtleties in lyrics*
- *A safe approach to dancing "Bahia Blanca" would be to walk confidently on the 'One' and the 'Three' and then collect and pause on the 'Four.' Walk again on the 'Five' and 'Seven' and pause at the 'Eight.'*
- *You can also choose to lead a pivot over the 'fill' at the 'Eight'*
- *Alternatively, make an arc or circle with your free foot or leg, during a 'fill'*
- *Knowing a piece gives you a distinct advantage with pauses*
- *Some teachers will use "-and-a-" and "tac, tac, tac" to represent Sincopaciόns*
- *You're never obliged to start on the 'One'*

- *But it's often easier to do so, as your partner is probably expecting that*
- *Waiting too long can feel awkward*
- *Even if the musical cues say "Carry on", you can still pause if you wish*
- *While there are ways to dance a tango that make more sense musically, there's no one "best" or "right" way to do it*
- *This allows you to dance to the same music for years, each time doing something different*

Chapter 7 Lyrics, Melody and Rhythm

> "There's something about the tango that brings even more emotion out of the lyrics." ~ Ruben Blades

Used in this chapter:
Songs
"Bahia Blanca" by Carlos DiSarli
Videos
"Highway to Hell" posted by 2cellos

"Bahia Blanca" is a remarkably polite piece of music. The Rhythm and Lyrics weren't invited and the Melody is passed back and forth between the violin, bandoneon and the piano. Meanwhile, the rhythm keeps trying to gate-crash the party.

Canaro's "Poema" is different.

The rhythm happily thumps along, while the melody and lyrics play around, gently stretching out some of the notes.

So in "Poema", do you dance to the rhythm or the melody?

Short answer - whichever you want.

Longer answer - it goes back to

"In my experience, about half of dancers predominantly hear the rhythm, a third the melody and a small number the lyrics. The remainder hear more than one of these." ~ Book 5

If you hear the rhythm, then you're going to feel more comfortable dancing to that. And so on.

Sometimes, in Argentine Tango - as in "Bahia Blanca" - you really don't get a choice; you can't dance to something that isn't there. To further muddy the water, often the degree of choice varies as the song progresses. In the Yuri version of "Poema", the beat is muted from 32 to 53 seconds, effectively forcing you to listen to the melody during that time.

This is why more experienced dancers often like to listen the music, before accepting a dance.

"I like this DJ, he consistently plays good music."

"The music has been good tonight; except for that tanda early on, which sounded more like 80s rock." ~ a conversation with a mildly, annoyed tanguera about the music played so far at a traditional milonga (dance venue.)

It isn't foolproof – a DJ can still start with a melodic song and then go straight into a rhythmic one. More experienced dancers tend to take note of who DJs in a way that they consistently enjoy. DJs who have a method of displaying the next tanda of songs, also make dancers' lives easier.

Precognition

"You don't believe in destiny?"

"Well, even if it does exist, I don't think I want to know. I mean, if every move we make is preordained, then what is the point of that? I mean, life is supposed to be a surprise." ~ Next

One of the issues in milongas is that less experienced dancers tend to just want to dance regardless of the music and so will try to sort out their next partner as quickly as possible in the cortina (break) between tandas (sets of songs, usually three or four.) This leaves those who want to dance to a specific kind of music to either accept a much smaller pool of potential partners, or take risks.

As most of us don't have precognition and can't accurately foretell the future, here are a few alternative solutions to this.

With partners that I know don't mind, I'm willing to dance against the music. If I know that a follower prefers to dance in a slow, melodic way and mid-tanda the DJ suddenly switches to a fast, choppy, rhythmic piece, I'll still dance it slowly and melodically.

If things get too bad, or you want to keep dancing with each other, but one of you positively hates this song, another option is simply offering to sit out that song – just sit down and chat; hopefully the next one will return to the feel of the first song.

You can just give up and possibly find someone to dance with who does like it. But be cautious - there's a fine line here between "there's no point suffering through this" and potentially insulting someone by finishing the tanda early, so again, I'd mainly reserve this for partners you know well.

'Call and Response'

When you understand it, 'Call and response' feels like it should just come under "Statements of the Obvious." Unfortunately, when someone does take the time to explain it, usually their "clarification" tends to be so over-complicated that it stops being useful and you just end up feeling even more confused!

If you've experienced one of the explanations of 'call and response' that made your head spin, take a breath.

Relax.

Exercise 26

Search Youtube for "2cellos highway to hell", posted by 2cellos.

Skip ahead to 45 seconds. The guy on the left, Stjepan plays a bit – the 'call' - and then starting at 11 minute 5 seconds, the guy on the right, Luka, plays back something different – the 'response.'

That's really all there is to it.

In this case, the difference is that Stjepan's 'call' is lower and it doesn't really change much. Whereas Luka's 'response' has a varying melody and is higher.

The response is mean to be an 'answer' to the 'call.' Here, the 'call' is Stjepan's lower phrase, simply because he plays it before Lucas' higher phrase.

The 'call' comes first; then the response follows.

Call –> Response.

There's a bit of overlapping between them in this piece, but for the sake of simplicity, just ignore that. At 1 minute and 38 seconds they both play the chorus. Ignore that too.

At 1 minute 56 seconds they go back to 'call and response.' However, this time they switch roles, with Luka first playing the steady 'call' and then Stjepan playing the higher-pitched melody 'response.'

"What's this I see, I thought this was a party? Let's dance!" ~ Footloose

Now things get interesting.

Stevie Vai joins in the fun at 2 minutes and 4 seconds. At its simplest, all that happens is that Stevie and Stjepan take it in turns playing the 'response.'

However, this immediately moves up a level and Stevie and Stjepan start responding to each-other as well!

This is where you get into the dangerous territory of making the whole thing so complicated, that it stops being useful.

So I'm not going to.

If it just occurred to you that Stevie and Stjepan are also doing 'call' and 'response' to each other, while they're each doing their 'response' to Luca - and that makes sense for you and helps you understand what's going on – great.

If that doesn't make any sense at all, you're better off not dwelling on it. Different people process musicality in different ways. The aim is to find the explanation that works for you, not to needlessly confuse yourself.

There's another chorus at 2 minutes and 30 seconds. However, halfway through there's a solo - the 'call' - from Stjepan at 2 minutes and 54 seconds where Stevie calmly rests his hand on his guitar, before playing his own solo – the 'response' - at 3 minutes and 9 seconds.

There's no set rule about how long a 'call' or 'response' have to be. It can be phrases, as we saw at the beginning. Or, as we've just seen, it can be entire verses.

At 3 minutes 24 they're all start playing - although Stjepan and Luka are now both playing the 'call' and Stevie the 'response.' The lines are now a lot blurrier with everyone playing continually. There's a musical cue at 3 minutes 40 – Stevie makes his guitar 'scream' and Stjepan throws up devil horns. This warns the audience, as if saying,

"Buckle up, here we go!"

Then everyone just cuts loose and has fun – 'call and response' goes out the window. Stjepan and Luka are playing the base melody and Stevie's playing another melody over the top of that, but there's no back and forth. Finally at 3 minutes and 55 seconds, the base melody also goes out the window and they all start playing intricate melodies, musically cueing the audience that they're building towards the dramatic ending. This song is not going to end on a gentle whimper of a note!

Light and Shade

"The Code is more what you'd call "guidelines" than actual rules" - Captain Hector Barbossa

Where do you draw the line of something still being 'call and response', especially when instruments start to overlap?

For social dancing, this works pretty well:

"Two different identifiable pieces of the music, played one after the other, that are still pleasant to hear and dance to."

As we just saw, they could be as big as the verse and the chorus. Or as small as a phrase and the 'fill' of notes after it. You can allow a little 'wiggle-room' for overlap, as long as you still feel there's enough making the two distinct from each other.

Performers often refer to this is idea as 'light and shade.' In a performance, if you just do the same thing for the entire song, no matter how well you do it, after a while it loses it's impact. By mixing things up, you keep things fresh and also gain more contrast. After a walk, a lift will usually be more dramatic than it would have been after yet another lift.

You can see this in Dancing with the Stars and

Strictly Come Dancing. In some dances, lifts are either prohibited, or only a small number are allowed. Here, the performers will tend to use as many as possible and even try to sneak in extras, knowing they'll probably gain more from the audience vote, than they'll lose from being penalized (if at all) by the judges.

But in the dances where they can legitimately do as many lifts as they like, you don't see them doing wall-to-wall lifts, because they know it's not as effective. Instead, they break up the "Wow!" moments with "tamer" steps, to give them more impact.

I know a couple who figured out how to do three minutes of continuous lifts, without the follower ever touching the floor – hence technically only doing "one lift" in their dance. The ruling body promptly changed the rules to reflect this, for the next competition!

This leads to an important parting of the ways between social and performance dancing. For a performance, you definitely want 'light and shade.'

But for social, it's more nuanced.

Imagine you're dancing with someone who hears the melody in the song. If you keep switching between the melody and the rhythm to create 'light and shade', but they're trying to interpret what you're doing solely through the melody, they probably won't enjoy it. They may also not even understand what you're doing. In which case you now have an unhappy and confused partner.

But for a song where the melody has a 'call and response', such as the above "Highway to Hell", and "Bahia Blanca" in the next section, then yes, creating 'light and shade' by dancing in a different way to the changing melody, can work well. Now your partner is able to interpret what you're doing solely through the melody, while enjoying the contrast that you're bringing to the dancing.

It's also worth noting that much in the way the different musicians took turns in playing the 'call' and 'response' to "Highway to Hell", it's possible for leader and follower to each choose one of these roles. For example, the leader may only dance the 'call', while the follower dances the 'response.' One way to accomplish this, is to take it in turns; whoever's role is currently playing, uses adornments and steps, while the other pauses and just uses weight changes if necessary.

'Heartbeat and Color'

Tango musicality exists in a state of tension between two points of view,

"Tango is the Compás"

"Tango is what happens between the Compás"

D'Arienzo put them together in this quote,

"Tango, for me, has three things: beat, impact and nuances."

One of my practice partners used to refer to the idea of 'heartbeat' and 'color.' For her, the 'heartbeat' meant the Compás and the 'color' was, as she put it, "All the fiddling around in-between the beats!"

In Terry Pratchet's "Carpe Jugulum", a vampire seeks to desensitize himself to holy symbols by repeatedly looking at crosses, ankhs, crescents etc. Unfortunately, near the end of the book, he has this revelation

"Everywhere I look, I see something holy!"

Religious symbols turn up everywhere, from crosses in-between window panes, to the crescent moon.

This is an important thing to bear in mind, especially with 'call and response' – after a while you can see it everywhere!

And it can become overwhelming.

I've had very simple dances that were mainly to the 'heartbeat' of the music. And I've had dances that were a riot of 'color!' You have to listen to your partner and see what works with them. It's like Goldilocks' and her porridge – too much... too little... perfect!

Ultimately, it's not about being "right", it's about this tool being useful to you. You get to draw the lines wherever suits you best, depending on how you and your partner hear the music.

Bahia Blanca

"Life has led me to other roads,
But, Bahía Blanca, I will not forget you."

While "Bahia Blanca" is terrible for learning to hear rhythm, it's great for 'call and response.'

Exercise 27

Listen to "Bahia Blanca" by Carlos DiSarli.

Again, I want to stress that there's no single 'right' answer to this.

One way to approach this, is to think of the first four seconds of higher notes as the 'call', followed by a two seconds of the 'response's' deeper, more pronounced notes. Followed by a 'fill' of piano notes. It loosely repeats at 9 seconds, only this time the 'call' is a bit longer.

It's a bit more obvious starting from 34 seconds where first the bandoneon plays the 'call' and then the piano replies with its 'response.' After this, the violin takes over playing the 'call.'

Alternatively, you could put the higher and lower notes together and consider the first 6 seconds as the 'call', with the 'fill' of notes afterwards to be the 'response'.

Or you could consider the whole of the song up to 35 seconds with the violins playing the melody to be the 'call' and then the next section up to 1 minute and 8 seconds with the bandoneon playing the melody to be the 'response.'

"Bahia Blanca" is a great song for playing around with this idea, which is part of the reason it's so popular as a performance piece – there's a lot of different ways to interpret where the 'call' and 'response' are, allowing for fresh new creations.

Exercise 28

Search Youtube for "Bahia Blanca performance."

Don't worry about finding any specific one, just watch some and see if you can spot how they've used this idea.

When is a Burger no longer a Burger?

Does there come a point where you've sufficiently moved away from 'call and response' that it's now something else?

This is a trap.

The answer is that for social dancers, it doesn't matter. The 'burger' is just to give you a reference point, not to force you to dance a certain way. Don't Shellac it and put it in a glass case.

Ultimately, you eat the burger.

And dance.

Sometimes, the music is just bad for social dancing - then you don't dance to it, much in the same way you'd consign a poorly-cooked burger to the garbage. Knowing how to recognize this is a useful skill for social dancing.

"I like music to have structure. Not nonsense. But not completely predictable either - not just boom-boom or thud-thud-thud." ~ conversation with a follower

But before you send the burger back to the chef (or complain to the DJ), bear in mind that some people actually like their burgers raw. It may be the DJ is playing something designed to cater to the other dancers. Something that may be mind-boggling to an inexperienced dancer, can be a great song to more experienced ones. Just as something that suits a less experienced dancer may be tiresome to more experienced ones.

And then there's the whole preference for melody, rhythm, lyrics...

But that doesn't mean you have to suffer through it. If you don't like your burger raw, go to places that cook it properly, the way you like. If you don't like dancing to something that sounds like elevator muzak, go to venues where you know the DJ will play music you enjoy dancing to.

Summary

- *If a song offers you both the rhythm and the melody, you can dance to whichever you prefer*
- *With an agreeable partner, you can dance against the music*
- *'Call and response' is just two different things, played one after the other*
- *Don't over-complicate it*
- *'Light and Shade' is a way of using contrast to prevent a feeling of "sameness"*
- *However, some dancers really enjoy a feeling of "sameness"*
- *'Heartbeat' and 'color' are a way of thinking about the beats and what happens in between them*
- *Find music that suits you. And DJs who play it*

Epilogue

> "It takes only one drink to get me drunk. The trouble is, I can't remember if it's the thirteenth or the fourteenth." ~ George Burns

As you make you way through tango musicality, dancing to the music can often feel a lot like helping a drunk friend to walk home. They're trying to go along with you and in the right way. But sometimes they stumble, or get entranced by something shiny, or want to stop and tell you about the time when they...

Fortunately, with experience, you start getting used to this and can keep everything going in - mostly - the right direction.

There will be some pieces of Argentine Tango music where you'll easily be able pick out the 'One', 'Five', 'Seven' and 'Eight.' The phrases and verses will be clear. You'll recognize the musical cues, and how they've used 'call and response.'

But others will feel like they had far too much to

drink! These are the ones that leave you wondering if you've actually understood musicality at all?

In large part, for social dancing this is the responsibility of the DJ. There's a good reason a lot of the same music is consistently played and a lot of music never gets any airtime.

When you're practicing, start out with pieces you find easier. If you get stuck, go back to the pop music examples in the book and give you brain and body some more time to tune-in to the more blatant musicality within them.

With time, you'll come to recognize if a piece is just too advanced for you right now – probably Biagi – or if it's just badly written for social dancing; if you like to dance to rhythm and the Compás, Piazolla's "Oblivion" is not going to work for you.

And that's ok.

Music is a powerful part of dancing. Finding what you like and how you like to express it in your dance is a valuable skill. It's fine if you don't like all tango music and don't want to dance to of it.

Yesterday, someone asked me

"Can you dance to music you really dislike?"

Yes, yes you can.

And a great many social dancers do. But, usually it's because there's a different pay-off. They may really want to dance with someone and this is the only tanda available. They may be happy to work on technique and tune out the music(!) They may simply be doing someone a kindness by dancing with them.

But dancing to music neither of you **understands**, is almost impossible. The only solution I've found for this, is to both agree to ignore it and instead dance to the music, or rhythm, in the leader's head.

At the end of the day, remind yourself why you like your friend enough to walk them home when they're drunk? Maybe they're a fun drunk? You might want to find some DJs whose tunes can better hold their liquor, instead.

Oliver Kent, Winter 2019

Statements of the 'Obvious'

"By knowing where the cues tend to punctuate music, you can reliably navigate by them, rather than having to memorize songs, or do math as you dance.

Just check for cues as you approach the punctuation points."

"To emphasize something, just do it in a different way to everything else."

"To emphasize notes, you can do the same things you do with words"

Terminology

Musical Genre
Music that belongs to recognizable group, or follows specific conventions, such as Jazz, Classical and Hip hop.

Punctuation
Musical cues tend to come in predictable places

Made in the USA
Coppell, TX
28 October 2020